Little
Tough Tips
On Marriage

Little Tough Tips on Marriage

Taka Sande

Little Tough Tips On Marriage
© Copyright 2013 by Taka Sande

ISBN 978 0 620 57482 2

For more information, please contact the author directly at:
Telephone: +27 (0) 72 324 2008
Fax: +27 (0) 86 602 5636
E-mail: admin@itsmyfootprint.com
Website: http://www.itsmyfootprint.com/
Postal: Postnet Suite 35, Private Bag X592, Silverton 0127, South Africa.

This book is designed to provide information about the subject-matter covered. Every effort has been made to make this book as complete and accurate as possible. However, there may be mistakes both typographical and in content. Therefore, the text should be used only as a general guide and not as the ultimate source of the subject matter covered.

Cover Design by: Tinodiwa Makoni, Harare, Zimbabwe.
Edited by: Greatness Factory Publishers, Harare, Zimbabwe.

Dedication

I dedicate this book to all those who are in need of restoration in their relationships, and to those making an effort to repair their marriages.

Welcome!

Putting your marriage relationship where it belongs!

This is what this book is about! Marriage is supposed to be fun and enjoyable. Every couple can have a fun and enjoyable marriage and they can have this if they are brave enough to pursue the *Little Tough Tips on Marriage*.

Marriage is a lifelong commitment that is made without an option to turn back. Marriage is like a garden that needs constant watering and great care. If you really love your spouse then your love is worth fighting for. This little book will revolutionise your approach to your marriage relationship. It will prepare you to navigate traps that can block the smooth flow of marriage, by reorienting your heart and attitude. The following tips covered in this book will help you improve your relationship with your spouse and will move your spouse from being an enemy to being your ally. This includes:

- Instantly cut your marital glitches in half!
- Aligning your priorities!
- Transparency and openness and,
- Handling both your spouse's and your quality lists.

Table of Contents

CONTENTS

Introduction

This book contains life or death advice, with do or die principles essential to enjoy your marriage and life.

Your children and your grandchildren's lives are at stake in your marriage. Actually the next generation of your offspring hang on the balance of your marriage. This is how serious we are as far as changing your future, through your marriage.

God takes family very seriously and so do we. Your family stands at the core of your blessed life here on earth.

In the beginning God did not make a church or cathedral, he made a family. In the beginning God did not appoint priests, or apostles, or prophets, or pastors, he appointed a husband and a wife. In Genesis, the first mankind gathering was a wedding ceremony, and not a worship meeting. After God, the next relationship that came was marriage. Surprising yet so true.

With these few words we offer you the complete and extended version of the *Little Tough Tips on Marriage.*

These are just tough tips on marriage. Where, when and how you choose to use this wisdom is up to you.

Enjoy it!

By Taka and Beatrice

You literally have the ability to change the future of your family tree through your marriage. Keep learning and advancing. Stay Inspired and motivated!

The way of a fool is right in his own eyes, but he who listens to counsel is wise. - Proverbs 12:15

Marriage or the relationship between parents dictates the stability of a family unit, and is to be valued as top priority.

The husband is qualified to lead his wife to the extent that he loves her!

1. How to Cut Half of Your Glitches Right Now!

Most people blame their spouses for the bad performance of their marriage. They never mention how much they, personally contributed to the bad performance or whether or not they played their part in the marriage effectively [Matt 7:3-5]. The bad behaviour of their spouse blinds them into believing that they are 'perfect saints'.

Your 100% Input Solves Half Of The Problems!

You are responsible for 50% of the performance of your marriage. This half comes from your 100% contribution or commitment to it. Research [Check Focus on the Family website] shows that any marriage in which at least ONE spouse gives his or her 100%, the marriage NEVER FAILS. Why? Well it is simple, if one spouse gives 100% and the other say 20%, this equates to an average of 60%, which is above 50%. Marriage fails when both partners start to give less than half the expected commitment. Here is how it is supposed to work.

Be Authentic!

First, be authentic! Any relationship that is not authentic is not stable and is likely to break up soon. If you pretend or fake to be 'good,' you will strain yourself and you will eventually get tired and subsequently reach breakpoint. So, purpose to be good to your spouse in a real way.

There Is Goodness In You

No matter how much your spouse has hurt you, remember that deep inside your heart resides a well of goodness. Tap into that goodness. Avoid paying evil with evil, but make a decision to be good to your spouse in spite of his or her short comings. Repaying evil with evil always doubles the problems and makes the situation worse. So repay evil with goodness. Remember you are the good guy, so be good.

Good Team VS Bad Team

If your spouse does something bad, do not join his or her team (the bad team). It does not make you a winner. Instead, remain in the 'good team,' executing your goodness with love so that you can win him or her to your team [Matt 5:43-47]. Many spouses make the mistake of 'declaring war' on their spouses, at the end they become guilty of being in the bad team as well. Do not team up with bad friends to fight your spouse. This does not make your marriage stronger. I repeat, 'fighting evil with evil does not build a good marriage,' but it actually creates a nasty one!' [1 Cor 13:1-8]

<u>You Control Your Happiness</u>

Do not be a victim of your spouse's bad behaviour. You control 50% stake of your marriage, but 100% of <u>your happiness</u>! Find good support and counsel. Engage or join a prayer group focusing on marriage and family issues. Again ladies, talking and spreading the word that your spouse is bad, does not help. Limit the people who know your horrible private stuff to only a few who pray with you. Increasing the people you communicate your relationship issues means that your energy is now focused on talking outside of your relationship rather than finding solutions. It will be painful when you discover that half the people at church are talking about you heart issues, and moreover that they are criticising and blaming you for your marriage problems.

Complimenting Is a Key

Praise your spouse and celebrate when he or she does good things. Complimenting, praising and celebrating are proven gestures of love that motivate people to continue to do good. This may include noticing what you admire on your spouse and telling them about it, bragging about your spouse, finding your spouse's Love Language and using it as a means to compliment him or her. Be your spouse's biggest fan and advocate. When you compliment, do it in a kind, sincere and honest way. Try to do it daily. Do not compare your spouse with other couples because he or she is not them.

Be Totally Committed!

Lastly, be committed to your spouse. I like the example of breakfast, with bacon and an egg. The chicken laid an egg for you to eat breakfast and she walked away. The pig on the other hand gave its life so that you could have the bacon. As far as this breakfast is concerned, the chicken was just INVOLVED but the pig was COMMITTED.

Be committed to love your spouse regardless of circumstance or situation. Be committed to build a happy, successful and fulfilling marriage. Commitment is 'no fun' but it is rewarding. Remember your commitment will be rewarded in due course [Gal 6:9].

Be bold, plan now to tie the knot! What's stopping you from wedding?

If you want to go deep in love, if you want real intimacy, then, live as if your loved one is more important than you, which means his or her interests becomes as important as yours.

Hear counsel, receive instruction, {and} accept correction, that you may be wise in the time to come. - Proverbs 19:20

A marital covenant is based on loyalty – 'until death do you part.'

2. Your 'Till Death Do Us Part' Promise!

It is you who promised your spouse *"To have and to hold, from this day forward, for better, for worse, for richer, for poorer, in sickness or in health, to love and to cherish 'till death do us part. And hereto I pledge you my faithfulness."* You made this commitment unconditionally!

So, stop blaming your wife or husband. Concentrate on keeping your side of the covenant or deal. When you do this, God will bless you, because you are obedient. If you cannot obey your own words, how can you obey God's Word? Stop expecting your spouse to be perfectly good or nice to you. He or she is not God. Neither is he nor she perfect.

On the day you made the promise, you did not say, 'If you stop loving me, I will leave you or if you misbehave I will ask you to pack your bags or if this or that happens, I will do this and that. No! No! You said, *"To have and to hold, from this day forward, for better, for worse, for richer, for poorer, in sickness or in health, to love and to cherish 'till death do us part. And hereto I pledge you my faithfulness."* This is serious stuff.

Keep your word, not just to your spouse, but also to GOD. If you do this, God's grace will cause your spouse to change. Stop trying to change your husband/wife because you can't. It is God who can, and before you ask God to change your husband or wife, make sure that you have kept your side of the marriage covenant, *"To have and to hold, from this day .... 'till death do us part. And hereto I pledge you my faithfulness."* The change that you want to see in your spouse will normally come after you change first.

This revelation will change you and your spouse. Stop being his or her 'policeman,' because it is simply not your responsibility. Just do your part and leave the rest to God. You did not marry your spouse to change or manipulate them. You married your spouse to LOVE them, come rain or come sunshine. This is what you must do. This is your primary commitment. This is your side of the deal. Think about this carefully.

Ground rules for success: Spend time with God and spend time with your spouse. Be a hero at home first before you become a hero out there.

You and your family are blessed, and you live to bless!

The man holds the key to successful marriage. The woman holds the key to happiness in marriage.

Love is not rude, it is not self-seeking; it is not easily angered; it keeps no record of wrongs. - 1 Corinthians 13:5

3. Who's First?

In this section we look at priorities in marriage, which must be as follows; 1) God => 2) Your spouse => 3) Your children => 4) Yours Parents => 5) Others including other people, work, church etc.

The Priorities

God is the supreme priority. He gets the first share of your time, relationship and income (tithe). You are to obey Him always. Period! After all you belong to him not to your boss, church or pastor.

Your spouse gets the second priority. He or she gets the second share of your time, relationship and income in fact he or she owns half of your possessions. You have to make him or her happy first before your children, parents, siblings or pastor. Actually, before God you and your spouse are one person.

Your children are in third position after your husband or wife. Your children have one father and one mother by divine appointment, so be there for them. Make your children happy, before everyone else. Spend quality time with them, parent them and do not delegate your parenting responsibility to television shows or the maid.

At fourth position are your parents. Regardless of circumstance we ought to respect them. Ephesian 6:2-3 [AMP] says, *'Honor (esteem and value as precious) your father and your mother--this is the first commandment with a promise. That all may be well with you and that you may live long on the earth.'* Note that your parents actually include your parents' in-law, so treat them as you would treat your parents because they are [Deut 5:16].

On fifth position is everyone else; siblings, cousins, aunts, church mates, colleagues, friends, etc. When one is single their priorities are different. God remains number one, parents are number two and siblings and everyone else are number three. However when one marries and has children, parents move down from number two to number four, and siblings move down from number three to number five. A lack of understanding of the changes in priorities when one marries and has children can result in parents and siblings competing with your spouse and causing animosity. Instead of your siblings interfering with your spouse and children, they must focus on their own spouses and children.

How To Treat Each One

Now, when praying, you pray for your spouse first before anything else, then your children, then your parents and then everyone else. Your spouse, children and parents must receive more prayers than anything else. When blessing, you bless your spouse first, then your children and then your parents, in that order, before anyone else [Eph 5:20-33].

Before you buy your pastor a suit, buy clothes for your spouse, your children and your parents first. This is what brings a *'sustainable blessing,'* not a takeaway kind of blessing. If you put the church before your family, you may get blessed, only to lose it because of the curse that comes from your mixed priorities. The church belongs to God, not to you; the pastor works for God, not for you; but your family is your primary responsibility by divine appointment. God takes care of his business, the church, and you should take care of yours, your family. When you take care of your family, God will bless you enough to be able take part in fulfilling Gods' mandate in the church. The Bible refers to the church as God's bride. You have your own wife or husband. God takes care of His, you should take care of yours.

The Blessing Begins At Home!

Don't put the cart before the horse! 'The blessing begins at *home!*' I am talking about sustainable blessing that is passed from generation to generation. As you gather at church the combined blessing can do much more bigger things because there is combined faith and blessing [Matt 18:19] but 'Prayer begins at *home.* God put Adam and Eve in the Garden of Eden as their *home* [Gen2:8]. It was a blessed home. There was no curse in Eden. This shows that our homes should be blessed. The primary place for experiencing God's blessing is none other than our homes. We safe guard this by putting our marital priorities in divine order.

Now, again *never* put your career or work before your spouse or family. It also brings a curse. If you neglect your spouse and prioritise your career you risk losing the extra money you get quicker than you get it. The promotion you get can easily turn into misery and bondage.

God's principal interest is to fellowship with you in prayer and His tithe, not to meet your daily list of demands that you call your prayer list. Free will offering, gifts, church building funds etc comes later.

Work and Other Activities Demands

Your second interest in life is your spouse's interests; not your boss's; friends or your work. Your spouse left everything for you. *You!* Not for your money or work. They gave up their identity for you. Hence you better be there for them. If you find yourself spending more time at work than with them, disaster will surely follow. Listen to the needs of your spouse, and meet those needs. Who will meet them if you do not? If the demand seems too big, then pray together about it. God normally intervenes. "If you and your spouse shall agree in prayer about anything, it will be granted!" [Matt 18:19]. The best team or agreement that can break any bondage or curse and cause overflow is a married couples' prayer of agreement. That's why the devil fights marriage.

Surprisingly you will find that each time you sacrifice these demands for your spouse or family, God blesses you. Each time you turn down some activity because of family demands, God will always compensate you.

You Have Two Choices!

You have two choices, either to go out sacrificing your spouse and family for your job or sport, working and toiling like an elephant but eating like an ant. Or you can choose your family and allow the blessing of God to work for you. Guys, *obedience* is better than *sacrifice,* because obedience is followed by the blessing. On the other hand sacrifice is associated with toiling! [1 Sam 15:22, Deut 28:1-2].

Agreement Brings The Blessing!

Husbands and wives, hear me on this, rather agree with your 'dull' spouse and receive God's blessing, than to argue and strife with an intelligent spouse and receive a curse. God works in a peaceful environment. It's better to lose the argument with God on your side, than to win the argument without God. Losing the argument with God puts the power of God in charge of the situation, thereby bringing to pass what you originally desired. Remember winning the argument has *nothing* to do with strengthening your marriage, but purely a display of ego.

True integrity begins at home. It begins with your relationship with your spouse and your children. Are you a person of integrity?

Communication is the core of any good relationship. And it is vital to communicate well within your marriage.

A fool gives full vent to his anger, but a wise man keeps himself under control. - Proverbs 29:11

A wife can build or destroy her husband.

4. The Quality Lists

In every relationship, for each one, there are two quality lists; 1) the **Good List** and 2) the **Bad List**. These two lists exist together and cannot be separated. Everyone or anything can have them. Knowing and understanding this can cure your relationship headaches. Let me explain ...

Definitions

1) **The Good List**; is a list of all the good characteristics or qualities you like or admire about your spouse. They are the reason that you chose him or her, why you or choose anything for that matter. They can include; honesty, confidence, kindness, humour, generosity, intelligence, good looks, success, loyalty, humbleness, creativity, frugalness, wisdom etc. Everyone likes to have a spouse with these qualities.

2) **The Bad List**; is a list of bad characteristics, qualities or the things that you do not like in a person or thing. Unfortunately they always accompany the good list. They may include being demanding, insecure, dishonest, judgemental, bitter, rude, selfish, failure, unfaithful, impatient, greedy, inconsiderate, foolish, etc. The bad list can never be empty because no one or nothing is perfect except God [Rom 3:23].

You Got Into This Relationship Because Of The Good List

You married your husband or wife based on the qualities listed on their good list. During dating, you actually tried by all means to supress the bad list to the point of convincing yourself to believe that it does not exist. Now that you are married, you realise that the bad list exists and is active. What do you do?

Focus On The Good List

Maintain the *dating time* attitude by focusing on the good list. Do *not* make it your mission to eliminate your spouses' bad list, because you will never achieve it. It can be equated to '*Mission Impossible*' and can only be achieved when your spouse dies. After all you also have a bad list. How big your bad list is depends on your spouse's opinion.

Every Person Has Two Sides

Every person has a good side and a bad side. However continue to focus on the reason why you married your spouse. Stop comparing yourself with others [Phil 4:11]. No two people are the same. God is the Lord of diversity that is why everyone is different. Life is not a competition. Everyone is unique and different.

They say the grass looks greener on the other side but you don't know how much it costs to maintain the greenery, or what lies beyond the attractive green grass. Who knows perhaps beyond the green valley there is *'Sodom and Gomorrah?'* Do not be easily swayed by green valleys after all you do not know how long they will last [Gen 13:10-11]. If the grass looks greener next door, it means they are watering it. Just water yours.

Appreciate What You Have

Love your husband or wife, kids, family, in laws, yourself and your country. You can like your car, house, job and everything about *you*. God made you, and put you where you are for a purpose. Do not listen to Satan and his friends saying anything to you that is in the contrary. If anyone does not like anything about you, it's their problem, not yours. You were called to where you are by God. Your failure to appreciate things is not God's problem. It is your duty to seek God and to find out what you are supposed to do with what He has given you. As you do this, you will start to find that *'all things work together for your good.'* Rom 8:28]. Even if your uncle is in prison or your spouse is a bit weird sometimes, 'all things work together for good'

Make It Part of Your Mission

I have personally summed up my life's mission as 'to enjoy everyday life and to fulfil my purpose.' I wake up every day and choose joy, and lots of it, as I do what God wants me to do. Some people like what I do, and some people do not. Well it's their problem. I have a mission and I am enjoying it.

So even when tragedy strikes, wake up to joy. Of course you can be sad for a few days if bad things happen close to you or to your heart, but after a week or so, wake up and eat your chicken; get back to business, go back online, enjoy everyday life and get back to what you were created to do. Smile as you go about your business [Phil 4:6-9].

Reckless words pierce like a sword, but the tongue of the wise brings healing. - Proverbs 12:18

Commitment means making a choice to give up other choices. It means to choose to make your marriage better.

Changing and keeping values is not an easy task, and it is not a one day job. Never the less, 'integrity starts at home'.

Watch were you go because, 'There is a way which seems right to a man, but its end is the way of death' - Proverbs 14:12

5. Transparency and Openness Matters

"Help, my spouse kept a big secret from me!" This is what you often hear when hidden marital issues are exposed. Many people believe that they can enjoy a great and fulfilling marriage, when they have closets full of dark secrets.

Transparency is a critical key in marriage and is mandatory for a happier marriage. Therefore, do not keep any secrets from your spouse and allow him or her to have access to all parts of your heart and life from the onset. This is the building block of trust and genuine bonding.

Key Transparency Areas

The following areas can potentially cause transparency problems in couples;

- **Phone or cell phone -** Can your partner answer your phone? Can your partner read the messages in your phone? Do you walk out of a room to receive a call? Any call or message that you hide from your spouse, compromises your relationship and anything that compromises your relationship is a potential risk.

- **Social media and email accounts -** Is your spouse your friend or follower on social media? Can you allow them to log on to your social media and email accounts without any fear? Is your spouse happy with your social media connections and comments?

- **Relationships, affairs and secret friends** – Does your spouse know your past relationships? Do you still communicate with your ex-boyfriend or girlfriend behind your spouse's back? Do you have secret friendships or relationships which you do not want your spouse to know about? Do you meet certain people behind your spouses' back?

- **Secret assets and finances** – Do you inform your spouse about *all* your earnings and tell them about unexpected earnings? Do you show them your payslip and bank statements? Do you spend money behind your spouse's back? Do you secretly give your relatives and friends money? Do you have secret possessions that your spouse is not aware of?

Marriage is a covenant and it is the only agreement that includes *total* disclosure. Keeping secrets from your spouse robes you of the peace that you need to enjoy your marriage. The guilt will consume you and make you uncomfortable. Instead of putting energy to have a better and happier marriage you will end up diverting that energy to hiding away stuff from your husband or wife.

You should not have secrecy on cell phone calls, friendships, emails or social media and your spouse should have access to all your accounts whenever she or he wishes. This is not comfortable given our ego, but it is one of the best ways to protect ourselves from immoral people and dark corners. Any person who is not comfortable to connect with your spouse is an enemy to your marriage.

Normally the things you do not want your partner to see are the things that can harm your relationship. If you really love your partner, then consider him or her as you post comments on social media. Make your spouse your greatest fan because you respect them.

Actually, on all the issues listed above, your spouse should have complete disclosure and you should not hide stuff from your partner. You are one and you share each other's heart. How can you say 'my heart is yours' when there are dark inaccessible corners inside? The strength of your commitment to your spouse is directly proportional to the depth of your disclosure.

Avoid A Long Distance Marriage Relationship!

Long distance relationships do not normally work well, simply because of the fact that it is difficult to love someone who is not physically present for a long time. Instead of becoming one the couple become two separate institutions, connected only by phone or perhaps social media. It becomes more like a *joint venture*, when it is supposed to be a *merger!* A relationship connected by phone or social media for a long time, without direct physical contact tends to get thinner and very fragile with time.

A woman or man leaves their family to be united with their spouse only to find that the person they sacrificed everything for is unavailable. This creates frustration and because of unfulfilled expectations, one spouse can begin to ask '*What am I doing here on my own? Why don't I go back to my parents, or maybe go out with my friends.*' On the other hand the spouse who has left home to earn an income for the family may feel content because he or she is sacrificing for the spouse and family back home. Because your spouse is not close to you, it increases the chance for other people to get closer to your heart. This door of temptation can cause you to get closer to other people and develop feelings for them, thereby compromising your marriage.

Research shows that the rate of HIV infection is higher in spouses that live in separate towns, and is even higher when couples live in different countries. [NCONGO; Kwena et al] Sometimes it is inevitable for couples to live in the same country especially when they live in countries that have economic challenges. Such scenarios will cause many spouses to consider leaving their partners and countries in search of better opportunities. This is ALWAYS followed by higher than average rates of divorce and separation. At times in your married life you will face a situation when you have to choose either more money or to be with your spouse. Choose wisely. In most cases you cannot have both. Many people especially husbands are blind sighted by the pain of poverty into taking lucrative opportunities away from home at the expense of their spouses and family.

Pray Together

Praying together and having family devotions together regularly, works very well. It is said that *'A family that prays together stays together.'* Family prayer time is not a place to dictate or deal with *unfinished issues*, but it is a time of love and oneness. Everyone must be free to participate and everyone's opinion must be considered. No one must dictate or force prayers. Normally the husband, as the family leader should facilitate or he can appoint another family member to lead. The Bible says *'when two or three agree ...,'* [Matt 18:19] this means the prayer of a couple in agreement is always answered.

Start Afresh

You might be having some challenges in the areas I have mentioned. Today, make a decision to change for good. Make a list of things you need to resolve and start changing them one at a time. Prayerfully engage your spouse as you rebuild your trust. This is important as trust is an ingredient found in love and it is the glue that builds a happy marriage. Start the road to healing your marriage now. It may not be an easy road, but it's for a worthwhile cause. *Do it for love! Do it in love!*

I made an agreement with my eyes. I promised not to look at another woman with sexual longing. - Job 31:1

We all want to be in love, to be missed, to be needed and loved. So, just love your spouse.

Apply Hebrews 10:24 that says, "As far as it be within you be at peace with all men," especially with your spouse.

The more sex you have, the better you marriage. As a couple try taking a 10 day 'sex challenge,' having sex each day for 10 day. The older you are the better your benefits.

6. Sex and Romance Basics

The three main common challenges in marriages are; sex, money and extended family. Dysfunctions in sex and romance are the number one marriage killers. Yes they are. Now in order to create a flow, I will focus mainly on husbands, because they are the leaders. They lead the 'dance,' and the wives respond.

First, let me remind you that any form of sex outside marriage is taboo. It is a sin and it brings a curse.

If you are married, then you have the right to enjoy it. The main question and challenge is how to maintain the spark of excitement and strong passion over the marriage years. Here are a few basic points:

1) Does the honeymoon have to end? No, it does not have to end at all. Keep the romance alive. Start dating your spouse again. You do not have to spend a lot of money in order to spend quality time with your spouse. Take a walk together, play games, share jokes and have fun together.

2) Unforgiveness and bitterness can choke the sexual intimacy. First forgive each other and create a good romantic atmosphere. Denying your spouse sex is just punishing yourself because you are putting pressure on him or her to look for it somewhere else. A fulfilled sexual life removes frustrations and releases endorphins (also referred to as the 'happy hormones').

3) Prepare, prepare and prepare. Make a habit of making yourself attractive for your spouse. Clean up, especially men, and a few women though. Look good and desirable. Brush your teeth and get rid of bad smells. Do it for someone you love. Always look your best, as a gift to your spouse.

4) Find out what excites her. Women don't get excited in a moment like men. It can take the whole day. Be romantic. Understand her love

language. Find out what makes her tick. For some women it's flowers, for some it is a romantic touch, for some it's just talking (quality time) and for some it's helping her with chores. This prepares the groundwork for her. When it comes to sex, they say a man is like a light bulb, if you switch it on, light comes shining brightly right away. It also switches off in a second too. On the other hand, a woman is like an iron, it takes time to heat up and it takes time to cool down. The iron is always hotter than the light bulb.

5) Talk about how you feel and what you like best. Listen to your spouse. If your spouse is happy, they will make you happy so focus on making your spouse happy. Communicate your desires and feelings to your spouse and listen to hers as well. Be genuine, do not fake it. The better the communication, the better the sex.

6) As you talk, explore, explore and explore. Discuss and try all sorts of new styles and positions. Do not be limited by the styles that you know. Be creative. Ask each other where and how you want to be touched and go ahead and do it.

7) Pray about your sex life, seriously. God created you, He knows you more than you know yourself. Ask for His wisdom and guidance regarding your sex life and how to improve it. Humankind may have discovered a few styles and positions but God designed thousands that are yet to be discovered. Try God for revelation and inspiration.

8) Have fun. Do not be too serious. Relax. Take your time. Sometimes it's not about getting there, but about creating a memorable journey. Arrogance is not romantic! Having sex with an egocentric person can feel like rape. Sex is about sharing.

9) As you take the responsibility of making your spouse happy sexually, you are sowing and you will reap and God will bless you. Every act of genuine service is blessed by God. Have an attitude of serving your spouse. Your acts of pleasing your spouse will be rewarded.

10) Lastly, *the grass is greenest where you water it.* Find good Christian books and material on marriage, sex and romance. Read together and learn together. Avoid pornography at all cost. It will affect your mind and your feelings towards your spouse.

A great man knows how to find a great woman, and vice versa.

The hard truth about accomplishing what you want as a couple; 1) an awesome plan, 2) and actually DOING the plan.

Get excited with life. Make a bucket list together as a couple.

Financial problems always affect and spill into marriage relationships. So make concrete plans to get out of debt.

7. The Right Spouse for Economic Success

An average millionaire is married with one spouse for a long period. Divorce, separation and strife in marriages tend to be economic liabilities. There is less divorce found among millionaires than the ordinary people. One can say 'because they did not separate, they became millionaires.' Divorce and separation not only cause legal fees, but they also cause loss of focus and reduce productivity.

Choosing The Right Spouse Is Critical For Success

I believe we all agree that the right spouse is critical for success. Studies show that, like most men, millionaire men said that 'good looks' were important when they chose their spouses. However unlike the ordinary men, characteristics like honesty, hardworking, sincerity, and love were also rated highly. Ordinary people first put emotions first before evaluating their choice. Economically successful people first evaluate their choices before making an emotional commitment, after all emotions tend to cloud judgement.

Having the same values and complementing each other is important. Complementing in terms of one spouse bringing in income and the other spending it does not work. Women in general are more likely to choose men who have a high potential of economic production. At the same time men feel threatened by high income wives.

People who marry someone because of wealth are often disappointed. The marriage is threatened when the spouse loses the source of income. Also people who marry someone only because of good looks are also often disappointed. With time the good physical features tend to evolve or even disappear.

How then can you find a good candidate for marriage?

How then can you find a good candidate for marriage? Where you meet each other has a lot to do with how the marriage performs. The chances of meeting a decent person in a bar are very low. If you want to meet intelligent single people, you go to a college or university function. If you want to meet a single person of Christian character, you go to a church youth function. And if you want to meet a generous person team up with volunteers.

Most millionaires' spouses do not have high paying jobs. Actually most do not work. They concentrate on running the home in an economic way.

Recently a wealth management consultant spoke to us. He said he had a client who came to him. The client is a senior police officer in his fifties. He had accumulated $2.7million over the years and wanted financial advice. On being asked how he accumulated all this wealth, given the salaries of civil servants, he said he saved 15% of every cent he and his wife received for the past 25 years. They put the money in good investments.

Economic Success Is Not About Going Beyond What You Earn

Economic success is not just about how much you earn. It is the ability to manage one's income through saving, creating extra income, investing, productivity, and of course the time factor. Your spouse will influence your decisions in these areas.

Some extracts from this article are from Dr Thomas Stanley's book 'The Millionaire Mind.' After conducting a detailed study of over 1400 millionaires, the results of the millionaire marriages proved that, your choice of a spouse plays an integral part of your economic success.

Stick with simple (and effective) investments, and avoid get rich quick schemes.

Fight debt, not each other!

You hold the key to everything you want for your marriage, your family and your life.

Money handled properly in marriage can be a source of amazing intimacy.

8. When You Married From A Wealthier Family!

Most men do not like the idea of marrying from a wealthier family. This is because it tends to threaten his critical role as the provider of the family. It can put pressure on him to perform financially so that his wife does not miss her former lifestyle and standard of living. As for her, coming from a higher lifestyle to a lower lifestyle is a huge challenge and a bold step of faith. In marriages this happens. Real love does not choose status.

You Might Be Getting Some Attacks

As a husband, if you are battling financially it tends to attack your self-confidence. Understand that she is coming from 'high to low' and that this is not your fault. Your wife may take it negatively, or she can choose to understand and move on with you. Your wife may resent you for her financial loss and pressurise you. Or she can choose to let go, and take it as a new lifestyle. You in-laws may even be the source of pressure, ridiculing you, belittling you or taking you for a joke.

Do Not Lose Hope or Be Desperate And Do Stupid Moves

In this situation, do not lose hope or be desperate and do stupid moves. This calls for wisdom. Win your wife first. Work through it together. All people start at the bottom (unless they simply inherit wealth) and build upwards. Take one *sustainable* financial advancement step at a time. Do not compare yourself with anyone. You and your wife are unique. You have created a unique family. Your in-laws took over twenty years to be where they are today, and you have just been married for perhaps only five years.

Few Words of Advice

Now here are a few words of advice on this;
* As a couple, accept each other's mistakes and learn from them. Identify each other's weak areas and find ways to complement them. This will help you create a strong team, become a winning couple.

- Pray together about your financial situation and read the word of God together. This synchronises your purpose, minds and hearts together. When faced with external pressure, keeping focus on the issues at hand is vital. As a family 'sing the same song' as you move towards a common vision.
- Seek good advice from experienced people. I often say that 'couples who often hide stuff, hoping to surprise the world by their success, are always surprised by their repeated failures.' Incorporating a wise friend can turn around your marriage and life. All the wisdom you need to breakthrough in life is already available through the people around you.
- Surround yourself with people who appreciate your strengths. Avoid people who speak words that attack your self-worth. Appreciate each other as a couple. Remember the key to your success lies within you strengths, not your weaknesses. So, identify areas your spouse is gifted in and encourage him/her to focus on them, knowing that your spouse's strengths have become your strengths as well.
- When visiting antagonistic family members, cut the visits short, pray a lot and plan before each visit. Do not take the bait and get into strife with them. Have the attitude of protecting your spouse from unscrupulous family members.
- Avoid 'get rich quick' schemes and scams. These days 'get rich scheme' are so well disguised, but you will know them by their super-normal promises of returns. Remember scammers do not carry a placard written 'scammer.' For centuries, the path and speed to sustainable wealth has not changed. It takes time, wisdom and hard work.

As you do this, know that your time will come, sooner or later. Keep building. You will make few or even many mistakes, but that's part if learning. Just keep building.

Beauty gets attention but personality gets the heart!

What you feed will grow! What you starve will die! Feed your marriage!

Comparing your spouse to someone else is a trap that will make you feel worse about your marriage.

Her children rise up and call her blessed (happy, fortunate, and to be envied); and her husband boasts of {and} praises her, - Proverbs 31:28 AMP

9. Attraction Is Just Attraction: Meaningful Relationships

If you want people to *like* something, create something *beautiful*. But if you want people to *love* something, create something people will *relate* to. With time beauty always fades but relations can get stronger. Unforgettable things are the ones that *touch peoples' hearts*, not what *caught their attention*. Human beings easily forget what *caught their eyes* but never forget what *touches our hearts*. So, try a little to touch hearts rather than impress.

Good looks are attractive but cannot keep you in your marriage! Good feelings make you feel good but do not make you stay!

Attraction is good because it draws our attention to something, so that we can investigate further. But our decisions to buy or get into a relationship or have long term engagement is not to be based only on the attraction, but rather based on how we relate to it! This is a wise way of making sustainable connections.

Building unforgettable things takes time and energy. It takes you inner most being.

Few of your close friendships will reach twenty years old. What will keep you connected with these few is not money or toys etc, it is the compatibility of your characters. Over the same twenty years you will have spectacular friends who will come, and go. Their characters did not really click with yours; and it's okay.

A good pay only attracts you to the job but it does not retain you! Good benefits look attractive but they do not retain you!

What makes a person stay for decades is how the work experience feels. That is why some people leave a good paying job to start a business. What do you think?

Do yourself a favour, forgive yourself of past mistakes.

Break destructive patterns that cause criticism and blame in your relationship.

Never make negative comments about your spouse in public. Instead praise him/her!

Live now as you build for your future. Love your spouse as if this is the last day. Do not postpone love.

10.   Did Your Spouse Change?

It takes time and effort to change, and it takes time for a spouse to believe that the positive change is real, and respond with his or her own changes. Whether we accept it or not, change is happening, for good or for worse.

If You Have Recently Changed In A Positive Way

If you have recently changed in a positive way, it may take a long time for your spouse to fully, 100% know you have changed for real and that you will not change back. This is not necessarily a lack of believing you, but rather a part of human nature that is very difficult to fight. Do not take it personally, do not confront your spouse about it, and do not give up. Remember that it is you who moved forward and is ahead, but your spouse can not comprehend it. You made the change first of all for your own sake, not just to please people. Keep going, keep growing and doing what you should, and wait for your spouse to catch up.

Lack of Quick Belief In The Change Can Discourage

Most people get discouraged by the lack of quick belief or appreciation from their family and quickly give up, going back way behind where they have been. You have to fight to maintain and defend you change. The environment will not make it easy. Instead find and hang around people who believe in you, people who can motivate you when your spouse is trying to push you in the opposite direction.

If It's Your Spouse Who Has Recently Changed

If it's your spouse who has recently changed, not being able to fully accept him/her change is beyond your control. However, you can work to control what you do and say. Verbally appreciate the change in your spouse. If you fail, let him or her know that you are trying your best.

It Takes Time To Trust

It takes time to trust, especially after incidents of disappointments. On the other hand, blind faith is even more dangerous. If you need more evidence and time to get assured that your spouse has really changed, go ahead and make sure. But do not disappoint your spouse in the process. Remember he or she has put a lot of effort in order to be where he or she is today. What your spouse needs is support, not a critic. The fact that he or she has changed means he or she knows that he or she was in the wrong path. Reminding him or her of the past does not make things better, but worse.

Let us not become weary in doing good, for at the proper time we will reap a harvest if we do not give up - Galatians 6:9

Take the risk today! Show how much you love your spouse! Be extreme about it.

Do not be too tense all the time. Soften up, have fun and enjoy your marriage!

Affirmation is awesome! Actually affirmation rocks! The power of positive words and gestures can turn around your marriage!

11.   How to Buy Presents For Your Spouse

How do you pick a present for your lover? For many people this is a difficult question. Having the genuine burning desire to please your spouse, and the thought of finding yourself unable to deliver what your feel can make one uncomfortable. As special occasions approach a lot of people go under stress wondering where to begin.

Each Occasion Calls for A Different Type Of Gift

Each occasion calls for a different type of gift; valentine, birthday, women's day, Father's day, anniversary, Christmas etc. although your husband would like a tool box, getting it delivered as a valentine present is not wise. Buying your wife a microwave or cooking pots for a valentine or birthday or anniversary does not sound right. But the same present on women's day is a great gift. The gift you get for your spouse is different from what you buy for your mother or aunt or any woman for that matter. Why, because a gift carries a message. It is a means of communication. And to the receiver, each present will always tell a story.

When should you buy your spouse a gift? My answer is 'you do not have to wait for a special occasion, but you must at every special occasion.' Your gifts to your spouse communicate your feelings towards him/her, so make them count.

Here Are A Few Tips

- Make gifts and presents a lifestyle. Do not wait until something unusual happens. There is no harm in reminding your spouse about your upcoming occasions and even your birthday.
- Avoid strife. If your spouse is not so excited about the gift, shoving it down his/her throat does not help.
- Be creative. Inexpensive gifts that create lasting memories are great. You do not have to purchase goods, something like a massage or movie can do him/her good.

- Know his/her love language and find the gifts around that. Make it an adventure as you try to unlock his/her heart.
- If necessary ask for help from a friend, or you can just google. Visit one or two marriage blogs for ideas.
- It is recommended to stay away from essential household goods as gifts, but try to make it personal.

I hope you enjoyed this.

Let us strive to live a life our children will be proud of, a life that is has a rich heritage. May our lives be a legacy to them and generations to come.

If not dealt with, debt can suck your emotional energy, lead you into crime, cause relationship breakdowns or even end in worse situations like suicide.

Your marriage is modelling a new culture for the future generations. As a Christian, the quality of your marriage relationship is related to the level of your faith. Actually your marriage is the display of your faith.

Cherish your spouse; decide to value your spouse as a priceless gift.

12. Running A Productive Home

"Somewhere along the line we stopped believing we could do anything. And if we don't have our dreams, we have nothing." Billy Bob Thornton as Charlie in the movie **The Astronaut Farmer**

Yes, *'a family that prays together, stays together.'* Yet I have discovered something even more profound that *'A family that dreams together is inseparable.'*

A family is a unit made up of individuals. In most cases a family is headed by the husband who is the leader, supported by the wife who is second in command and lastly there are the children. It is a team were one is born into. Upsetting the functionality of a family leads to serious physical and emotional losses to its members.

A family does not exist, apart for a reason. It is important to find your family's purpose. This may involve individual soul searching; identifying what you want as a family (vision); what you stand for (values); what you are good at or what you have (resources). These things bring fulfilment into families.

Some of the most important issues in a family are integration, consultation and good leadership. The husband is by nature the leader and his role is to support and advance the cause of his team. He protects the members and stirs the course on behalf of the family. Being authoritative normally leads to his down fall and subsequent loss of his most needed pride. On the other hand being docile and passive, creates even more problems. John Maxwell sums it all by saying that 'everything rises and falls on leadership.' This includes families!

Vision

A family without a vision is of course going nowhere. At the end family members will start to look for their purpose somewhere else. Develop a vision and write it down. A family vision is simply a dream of where you see the family in five, ten, twenty or thirty years. The vision can be broken down into sub-visions and goals covering specific areas. Allow each family member to participate in the implementation or roll out of the vision in order to get buy in and support. Track progress and give feedback.

One of the most inspiring movies I ever watched is 'The Astronaut Farmer.' I particularly like Charlie's father-in-law's words when he said, "I couldn't get my family to eat together. (But) You have your family dreaming together." It was indeed a crazy dream. The idea of Charlie, an ordinary farmer, making a rocket and managing to take it to space, despite opposition from banks, the community and even the government, is really amazing. His family members were joined in this vision and were prepared to make sacrifices to see it happen. This shows what a family with a single dream can achieve. Nothing can stop a family united in a dream.

Marriage

Marriage or the relationship between the parents dictates the stability and foundations of a family unit, and it is to be valued as top priority. On a long term basis, trust and honesty becomes more important than physical features of the couple. Remember once trust is broken, it is not easily restored but it is not impossible either. Be a person of integrity and keep your vows. A successful family helps each member to realise his or her dream. Selfishness brings frustration to family members.

Values

Values go from top to bottom. The parents' values become the children's values. A study in schools in Pretoria East's low density suburbs really shocked many. 82% of the children admitted that they have at least once seen their parent bribing someone. Above 50% said it happened more than once. These are the so called affluent suburbs where managers and leaders live. These statistics say a lot about the current leadership and the seed that has been sown to the children.

Changing and keeping values is not an easy task and is not a one day job. Nevertheless 'integrity starts at home'. The reason why our nations are in a mess is because there is no integrity at home. We are nice angels in church and devils at home. We criticise leaders or relatives right in front of our children and expect the children to respect the same leaders and relatives. If you bad mouth your pastor or church in front of your children, how do you expect them to obey them? It is even worse when parents fight in front of their children.

Children

Children follow parents. They do not do what you say, but what you do. So forget about giving them a lot of lectures, *'just do it!'* Remember every child is looking for a hero. If they do not find one in the home, they will look somewhere else. Be their role model. Spend time with them. Kids do not really want toys, 'they want you.' Do not ignore them, otherwise they will find someone who will not ignore them and it is not going to look good if the bad guy next door gives your kids the attention they need. Kids follow people who give them attention.

Create good memories for your children. I mean you would not want the kids to remember their father as the guy who watched TV all the time or was never at home. If you do not teach your children, the TV will do it for you. Is this what you want?

On the other hand, kids need to be disciplined. Give and define for them rules to follow and boundaries to keep. It gives them a sense of identity and security.

Family Systems

Run the family using wise principles. Put up economic and social systems; and principles to handle your family as well as your extended family. Introduce systems to run your finances and home. Have systems to deal with friends, systems to deal with health etc. If there is anything you are going to do a number of times is putting systems in place. Agree on these systems and adjust them as you go.

Systems take you out of the constantly endless decision making processes. They save time because everyone knows how things are done. They ensure consistency and hence enforce fairness. Even if you are not around your spouse or kids will know what to do. Families with a common vision and fixed systems have fewer arguments or blame games. Normally systems are made in a sober environment long before the critical situation comes.

Systems should reflect your values, goals and environment. They must be fair and should be adjusted with time. With time systems will define your culture and identity. Clearly defined systems are a good tool for controlling the family. As a family, if everyone behaves as they please or if they are forced to behave in a certain way, failure is highly likely.

Family Finances

Like a business, each family needs to manage finances well. Each family has an **'income statement'** or a budget. A budget is not just a planning tool but a system to control finances. The income statement shows *all* your earnings, expenses or savings for a given period, in most cases it is shown monthly. It is not wise to spend more than you earn, because you will end up having to borrow. Aim to save and invest at least 10% of your income. Put it in secure funds or investments. Ask for advice from trusted experts or even study a bit on personal finance. A $10 text book on personal finance can save you a lot of money and change the course of your family finances.

A budget normally has the following items;
1) Non-negotiable or fixed expenses: rent, taxes, insurance, food, transport, car and house payments, church or religious giving etc.
2) Retirement: Money set aside into pension fund etc.
3) Long-term savings: Money set aside for car purchases, major home renovations, or to pay up substantial debt loads.
4) Irregular expenses: major repair bills, new appliances, etc.
5) Fun money: Money set aside for entertainment or holiday purposes.

A family **'balance sheet'** is increasingly becoming an important document. It is a statement of everything you own as well as your credits. It lists current assets such as cash in bank or investment accounts, long-term assets such as shares and real estate, current and long term liabilities (what you owe) such as loans, mortgage and other forms of debt. Securities and real estate values are listed at market value rather than at historical cost or cost basis. A **Family's Net Worth** is the difference between the family's total assets and total liabilities. This is normally used to measure how wealthy the family is.

Being wealthy does not necessarily mean having big figures on your budget, but rather the value of the assets you have accumulated over time. You can increase your wealth by ensuring that your expenses are less than your income, as well as by saving or investing the difference between your expenditure and income. Many families have huge budgets but little net worth because of over expenditure.

A happy marriage is based on friendship. In life, good friends are hard to find, the same in marriage. Aim to become better friends as husband and wife.

Transform your home from a 'war zone' to a place of peace and love.

"Behind every great man there is a great woman." As you bring out the very best in each other, the two of you can become a powerful team.

Aim to create a passionate sexual relationship that meets your spouses' and your needs.

13.   Final Nuggets On Marriage

In this section I will share with you a few nuggets on marriage.

When Conflict knocks at your door

Major sources of marriage conflict like domineering in-laws, wayward children, stepchildren, finance, sex, friends, cultural upbringing, time apart and expectations, can easily turn a happy home into a war zone.

Most of these issues can be avoided and resolved by good communication, forgiveness, setting up and drawing up boundaries, understanding and defining the problem, pursuing purity of heart, setting and agreeing on priorities, planning a time (and place) for the discussion, affirming your spouse that you relationship is first priority, sticking to the issue and proposing a solution. Revise your resolution after some time and adjust accordingly.

Keep Reconnecting A High Priority

Most couples begin their marriages with great excitement and expectations. With time, however, life's demand and stresses begin to take their toll, demanding your time and your energy. In addition, the arrival of children typically brings greater stress, pushing husband and wife further apart.

Connecting has to be put on high priority for couples. Find ways to remain connected while negotiating the real circumstances of life.

The Case Of Unfinished Business

The best gift you can give your spouse is not money or good time or anything, but a husband/wife with a good heart or without 'unfinished business.'

'Unfinished Business' - includes the following; unforgiveness, childhood fantasies, inferiority complex, low self-esteem, pride, anger, fear, greed, selfishness, coldness (that is, not showing emotions), judgemental, rejection, depression, fornication, stubbornness, hurt, withdrawal, , aggression, insecurity etc, these things normally develop due to past abuses or through the environment we grow up in this rough world. And these should be dealt with if one is to fully enjoy his blessed life as a good husband or wife. These things do not disappear. I repeat again, these things do not just disappear. They change from one form to another depending on the environment. They must be dealt with viciously.

Addictions, strife and other marriage issues normally come through this door of 'unfinished business.'

Leading by Example

'If we fix all the women in this world, half of the problems will be solved. But if we fix all men, 100% of the world's problems will be solved.' Why, because men are at the top. They lead families. Sustainable change starts at the top, with the head of the household.

Men who 'send' their wives to church to be 'fixed' get a sudden relief when the wife changes, but he soon loses when the wife gets frustrated by the untransformed husband. Contrary to this, if a right standing man of the house says, 'This is how things will go in this house,' the whole household will line up to that and follow.

Men, remember your household will not do what you say unless you yourself do what you say. If you use double standards, your wife and children will also find areas to use double standards.

You are the head. You determine the direction, the course and the quality of your household. Integrity begins with the husband.

Family Devotions

Husbands; as the priest of the family, men have to frequently initiate family devotional or prayer meetings. You do not have to lead everything, just facilitate by appointing who does what. Be creative and interesting. Keep it simple. Avoid dictating or boring meetings or being selfish. Give everyone a chance to participate, from small kids, teenagers to even non-Christian family members. Remember there is no perfect family devotion. One of the main purpose is to have fun in love, to come together, learning and developing. If one prefers lengthy prayers he/she can do it in private.

Choose to have these meeting at intervals that work well with your family. The most important thing is that you have to do something. Let us unit our families as we facilitate prayers or bible study at home.

The Golden Asset

One day a poor farmer was moving around in the farm doing his business when he came across his lovely goose. Upon looking he saw that the goose had laid an egg that looked like gold. He threw it away wondering what is was, but on second though he picked it up and took it to town to be tested. Well, he found out it was pure gold.

Next morning he went to his dear goose, only to find another golden egg, and took the egg. Every day he started to pick a golden egg. With time he became very rich. And as he grew richer so did his greediness.

One day he said to himself, 'if I can kill the goose and reach inside and get all the golden eggs at once.' He went on to follow his plan, only to discover that there was not a single egg inside the goose.

Now what is the story all about? The goose is your marriage relationship or asset and the golden eggs are the benefits or products. This situation happens in relationships, business, work life etc.

If you focus and get concerned with the golden eggs and neglect the asset, soon you will not have the products. At the same time if you get concerned with the asset only and not get the benefits, a time will come when you won't have any motivation to maintain the asset. Actually you may end up asking yourself why you are maintaining the asset.

In my words I would say 'keep the asset happy and you will have a golden egg every day.'

Many people neglect to maintain the asset and eventually lose their marriage, relationship, business, etc. In short, if there is something you are getting benefits from, keep that thing happy. And you will be happy for a long time.

Marriage Is A Marathon

Marriage life is not like a sprint that takes a few seconds, but it is like a marathon that takes hours. It is a commitment that last a life time.

Athletes know that you cannot afford to be thirsty when running. In a marathon one has to keep drinking water constantly. If you drink when you are thirsty, it's too late. So you drink before you are thirsty.

The same in marriage relationship, you have to keep on replenishing the relationship. Do not wait until you see cracks in your relationship, it will be too late. So, take action today. Find marriage resources, attend marriage seminars and keep improving your relationship before cracks appear.

Seeking help when the marriage has fallen apart is 'good.' Seeking help the moment you see cracks is 'better,' but constant replenishing your relationship to avoid cracks is the 'best.'

As You Resolve Conflicts With Your Spouse

'Submit to one another out of reverence for Christ' (Ephesians 5:21):

- The environment, pressures and conditions around you matters. Choose to resolve issues in private when you are emotionally positive and you mind is sound; not when you are hungry, in a hurry or under any pressure.
- Avoid finger pointing. Start your sentences with "I" instead of "You." For example "I feel frustrated when we are late" is easier to hear than "You always make us late," because the latter is finger pointing.
- Keep your fighting away from your kids, unless you intentionally want to model how to resolve it in front of them.
- Stay clear of 'character assassination' and name calling. Do not assign negative labels to each other (e.g., 'You're so lazy'), because this is name calling, and not helping to bring a solution.
- If you need a break from the discussion, take it, but agree on when you will come back. This helps you to rethink, refocus and cool the tempers, and perhaps seek God about it.
- Avoid expressing contempt by rolling your eyes or being sarcastic. It is toxic to your relationship. It sends the message that 'whatever you say, I won't listen. There is no point in talking to you.'
- Think win-win, not win-lose. Take the path that makes you better as a couple, than the path that make you the winner and your spouse the loser. You are a team. Choosing to win over your spouse is a sign of selfishness.
- Focus on solving the problem at hand, not what happened 20 years ago. Focusing on the past does not take you forward. That why you have to forgive and forget the past before engaging about the future.
- Spend most of the conflict resolution time trying to see the world through your spouse's eyes. Seek to understand before being understood. This make a big difference and quickly brings the conflict to an end. Your spouse is not your enemy out to get you, but your ally.

Social Media Can Ruin Your Relationship

Pornography, chat Rooms, cyberSex and the like can ruin your marriage. When you engage in these, your spouse will fell 'cheated,' robbed of some part of their marriage. Have a clear discussion on these issues with your spouse in order to agree and establish common boundaries.

Social Media, that is, Facebook, Twitter, MySpace, Instagram, Chat Rooms, Snap Chat, MixIt etc also have the potential to damage your marriage, if not handle properly. Generally, if you wouldn't say it or type it with your spouse watching, it's probably not something you should be saying or typing. If it really is as 'innocent' as you keep telling yourself that it is, it would not matter who was around or reading it.

The way you listen to your spouse and children says a lot about how you listen to God. - Phil Zaldatte

Sometimes it's how you say it that really matters.

Make it your ambition to create good memories for your spouse and children.

Reckless words pierce like a sword, but the tongue of the wise brings healing. - Proverbs 12:18

14.   At The End Of The Day...

Life is about having fun. Have fun with your spouse. Have fun with your family. Aim to enjoy each moment.

Just like life, marriages go through challenges. Some caused by human actions while others by nature. Be patient with each other as you work through the issues at hand. Counselling can help to dissolve problems especially if both members are willing to be helped. It is unfortunate that couples silently go through challenges in their marriages until they divorce without sharing their issues with close friends.

You need each other more when are having challenges in conceiving a child. In this case the husband must be very supportive of the wife. Try by all means to live a fulfilling life. Absence of a child is not absence of life. Gather and associate with people who understand and support you. Be ready to forgive, especially those who do not understand your situation. As you pray and seek God, there is no problem in considering adopting a child. Formal adoption is preferred and the younger the orphaned child the better. God work in mysterious ways!

As you live, seek to fulfil God's calling and purpose in your life. God designed all things for a reason. Find what He wants with your life. As you follow His plan, he will guide you and strengthen you all the way.

My advice is not cast in concrete, neither is it a *one size fit all*. Try and see what works for you.

Beatrice and I wish you an awesome marriage!

Ask yourself every day, "What can I do today to make my spouse and family happy?"

As a woman, you hold the keys to unlocking the goodness in your man and to shut it down! Use these keys wisely.

Love is a choice, that's why we are commanded to love. Love is a commitment, not a feeling. Choose to love your spouse!

A Prayer For Change

Heavenly Father, I come to you in the name of Jesus. I pray and ask Jesus to come into my heart and be Lord over my life. I confess that Jesus is Lord, and I believe in my heart that God raised Him from the dead. Forgive me of my sins and make me your child.

Father, I pray for my marriage. I ask you to change my heart and make me able to love my spouse the way you want me to. Heal my heart and my marriage from the past hurts. Fill me and my marriage with your love and help me to accept my spouse. Give me wisdom to pursue and resolve issues in my marriage. In Jesus' Name. Amen!

About Me

My name is Taka Sande. I am an author, teacher of the Word of God and a social and economic entrepreneur who facilitates social, spiritual and economic development. I am also the creator and Managing Editor of www.itsmyfootprint.com blog. I have been a church leader for over 15 years. I fellowship and serve as a leader at Hatfield Christian church, www.hatfield.co.za in Pretoria, South Africa.

I have a passion for making a difference in the world by influencing and adding value to people's lives. I really believe in living a result orientated and purpose driven life. I enjoy facilitating processes that advance and improve the lives of people, spiritually, socially and economically. I also enjoy helping people find their purpose, maximize their potential and reach the limit of their calling.

I love my wife Beatrice, and we have three children Tanya, Tinashe and Israel.

You are welcome to connect with me at It's My Footprint on:
- Email - admin@itsmyfootprint.com
- It's My Footprint Blog - http://www.itsmyfootprint.com/
- Facebook Group - https://www.facebook.com/groups/174721272602912/
- Twitter - https://twitter.com/ItsMyFootprint
- The Awesome Marriage Guide - http://paper.li/f-1312641338
- Little Tough Tips on Marriage Facebook Page - https://www.facebook.com/LittleToughTipsOnMarriage

My Other Publications

The Discipleship Series

If you really want to enjoy your Christian life, this is the book to read. This book provides basic foundational Christian life principles. It is a great tool for personal Bible study, and to grow in the knowledge of God. This book is available on Amazon or you can get more information on It's My Footprint website.

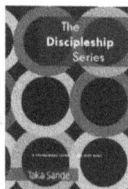

The Blessing Scriptures

This is a compilation of blessing scriptures that will inspire and motivate you, to live each day in faith, peace and joy. Meditating on these scriptures builds ones faith. This book is will be available soon on Amazon or you can get more information on

It's My Footprint website.

It's My Footprint Newsletter

This is an inspirational newsletter that offers wisdom for life. You can subscribe for *free* to It's My Footprint Newsletter at www.itsmyfootprint.com.